CW00385873

Spirit of Jersey

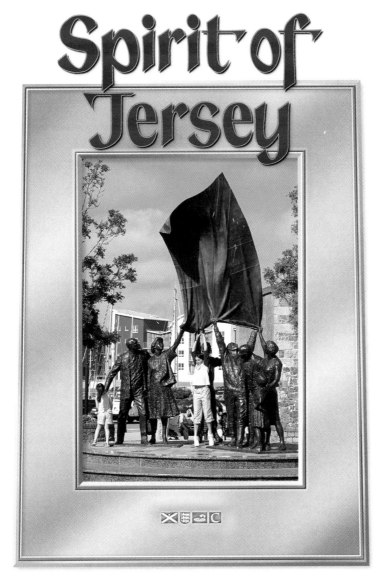

A PHOTOGRAPHIC PROFILE

Photography	**Michael Thompson**
	Miles Cowsill
Text by	**Philip and Marion Falle**
Designed by	**Tracey Harding**
Published by	**Lily Publications Ltd**
	PO Box 33 Ramsey
	Isle of Man IM99 4LP
Telephone	**+44 (0) 1624 898446**
Fax	**+44 (0) 1624 898449**
ISBN	**1 899602 02X**

Lily Publications
LIMITED

1

I am pleased to have the opportunity to contribute the foreword to this book celebrating the character and the history of our unique Island.

Jersey may be an island of only 45 square miles, nearly 100 miles from the south coast of England, but it has played a role disproportionate to its size in the history of the British Crown. Part of the Duchy of Normandy at the time of the Battle of Hastings, Jersey remained loyal to King John when the English Crown surrendered to the French army its possessions on the neighbouring Cotentin peninsula.

Over the centuries since then the Jerseyman has been able, on a clear day, to look across the narrow stretch of water that separates him from nearby France in the knowledge that his loyalty to the English Crown gave him not only the protection of the Monarch against invasion but also special privileges that persist to this day and define Jersey's character.

Some of the landmarks around the Island tell their own stories of the struggles he has faced. During the English Civil War the future King Charles II took refuge in Elizabeth Castle as the conflict raged in England. The Royal Square in 1781 saw the Battle of Jersey in which British forces fought off invaders from France, and in the many fortifications that ring the coast, the legacy is still visible of nearly five years of German occupation from June 1940.

Today these are chapters in our past but they help to explain the curious mixture of independence of spirit and loyalty to the Crown upon which Jersey's prosperity is built. From it have emerged institutions adapted to the modern world – the States of Jersey, our own democratic parliament, and the Royal Court, the Island's independent judiciary.

I hope you will enjoy discovering more about the Island in the pages of "Spirit of Jersey".

Sir Philip Bailhache,
Bailiff of Jersey

Coutts (Jersey) Limited,
PO Box 6, 23-25 Broad Street, St Helier, Jersey, JE4 8ND
Telephone: 01534 282345

Jersey Tourism
Liberation Square, St Helier, Jersey, JE1 1BB
Telephone: 01534 500777
Fax: 01534 500808
www.jersey.com e-mail: info@jersey.com

Commodore Ferries (C.I.) Ltd
PO Box 10, New Jetty Offices, White Rock, St Peter Port, Guernsey, GY1 3AF
Telephone: 01481 728620
Fax: 01481 728521
www.comferries.com e-mail: enquire@comferries.com

Acknowledgements

The publishers are grateful to the following for their assistance and research with this title:

Dave and Ann Hocquard; David Jandron; Rozena Newell; Jeff Vidamour (Commodore Ferries); Mike Sunier (Chrystal PR); Michael Tait (Jersey Tourism) and Douglas Creedon (Jersey Tourism).

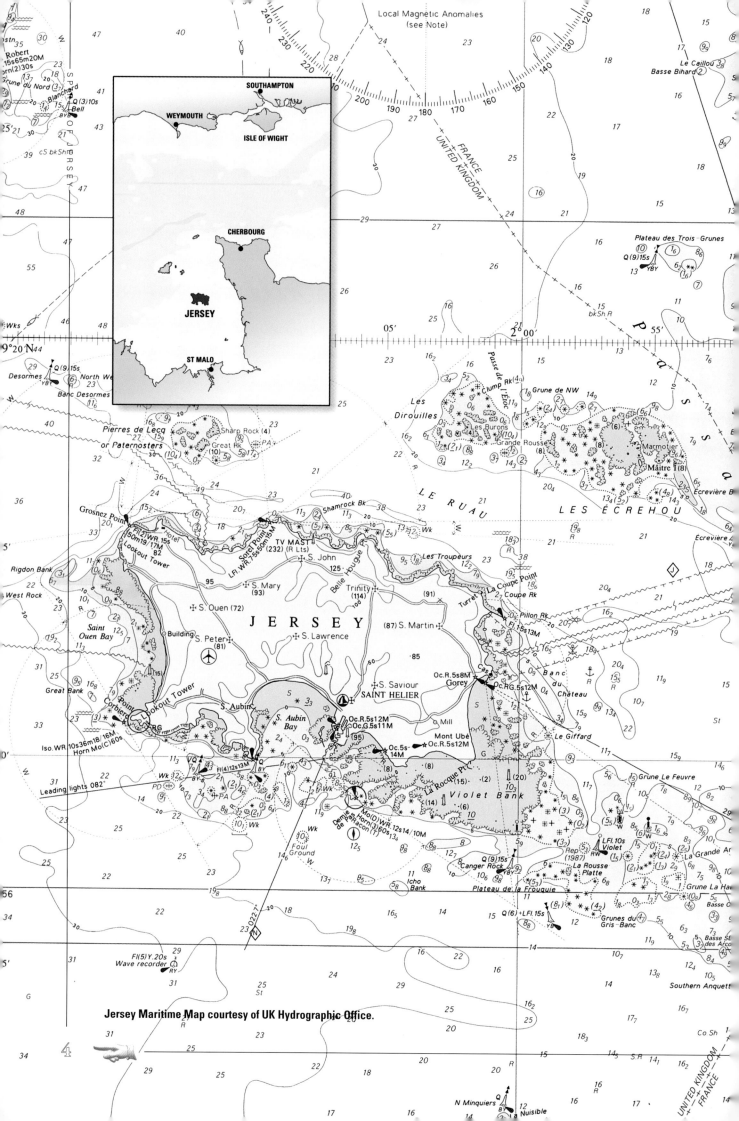

Jersey Maritime Map courtesy of UK Hydrographic Office.

Early Jersey

Jersey has not always been an island. As a plateau overlooking more northerly sisters which became the other Channel Islands, it was part of the great continent of Europe.

The magnificent sweep of St Ouen's Bay, the Atlantic seaboard which forms the west coast, provides evidence, if not of union with the Europe then certainly of a much larger island. At low tide (it rises and falls over 40 feet on occasions) peat beds and tree stumps are visible. This forest, predominantly beech, oak, alder and hazel, is probably about 7,000 years old.

Jersey's traceable history really begins in the Old Stone Age and signs of man's occupation have been found in the internationally renowned excavations of La Cotte de St Brelade and La Cotte à La Chèvre. Historians suggest a date of some 250,000 years ago but that is for the specialist. For this brief snapshot, the arrival of Neolithic colonists in about 4000 BC is the logical place at which to start.

They were settlers and to them Jersey owes its wealth in the dolmens which were their tombs. The most outstanding example is La Hougue Bie, one of the finest Megalithic tombs in Western Europe, which was bought in 1919 by La Société Jersiaise, the archaeological and historical society.

This and other tombs suggest a population able to haul huge blocks of stone, some weighing 30 tonnes, considerable distances. Their design, particularly La Hougue Bie, also indicates a sophisticated community. Twice a year, at the vernal and autumnal equinox when days and nights are of equal length, a pinprick of light from the rising sun strikes the rock at the rear of the tomb, within minutes bathing the chamber in an orange glow.

Later came the Bronze Age and its most notable artefact is the magnificent gold torque found by workmen in 1889 when digging foundations for a house. Now owned by La Société, it is composed of 140 centimetres of gold, twisted into a four-flanged spiral bar. It weighs 746 grammes and is so valuable that only a replica is displayed in the Jersey Museum.

The Iron Age brought further invasion from mainland Europe with the arrival of the Celts, or Gauls, and thousands of their coins have been found at various sites. The Romans followed but, perhaps surprisingly, given that their work has endured elsewhere, no confirmed trace of a Roman building has yet been found.

It is from then that Jersey's ancient name of Caesarea originates, with Guernsey as Sarnia and Alderney as Riduna, although there is considerable dispute as to the accuracy of this.

The Jersey flag

Christianity and the Martyrdom of Helier

In the absence of documentary evidence, no one is certain how or when Christianity was brought to Jersey. The 17th century historian Poingdestre wrote: 'As for Christian Religion it is not easy to marcke precisely the time of its first beginning in these islands, for questionlesse it came not all at once, by a Generall Conversion, noe more than in other parts.'

However, there is little doubt that the 12 parishes have existed for many centuries. A view exists that the central parishes of St Lawrence, St John, St Peter, St Saviour and St Mary originated in around 475. A 20th-century historian has pointed out that in Coutances, in nearby Normandy, a bishopric was established in the 6th century, while St Maglorious's monastery in Sark dates to about the same time.

According to legend, Helier was a hermit murdered by heathens in 555. His saint's day is 16 July, commemorated with a pilgrimage across the causeway to the hermitage at Elizabeth Castle where he is said to have lived. Jersey's principal parish bears his name.

An inscribed and decorated stone suggests that a church or chapel existed where St Lawrence Church now stands not long after Helier's time, perhaps as early as the beginning of the 7th century. Corresponding evidence in Guernsey of about that period might indicate the existence of parishes – the beginnings of the 12 ecclesiastical and later civil municipalities which exist today.

Each parish has a shoreline, although in St Saviour it amounts to no more than a few feet at The Dicq where it meets the boundaries of St Helier and St Clement. A possible explanation is what in Norman times was known as the Franchise de l'Eglise – a right of sanctuary in Norman law held by the parish churches.

In addition, sanctuary paths, known as perquages, were also established and these led from the church to the sea. Criminals seeking sanctuary from the law used these paths to leave Jersey and part of one – appropriately named Le Perquage – still exists, leading from Sandybrook in St Peter's Valley to the coast near Beaumont.

The Normans and their remaining influence

Jersey owes much to its Norman ancestry, not only its language – Jèrriais, or Jersey Norman-French – but also some of its legal system.

The Vikings started their emigration southward in about the 9th century and some settled in the part of Gaul now known as Normandy. In 911 Rollo, hitherto an area chief, was recognised as Duke of Normandy.

A legal relic of those days remains today. The Clameur de Haro is said to date back to Rollo's day and can be invoked by anyone believing their property is threatened. An example is perhaps that of a landowner who believes a tree he owns is being felled by a neighbour.

In front of witnesses, the aggrieved person kneels at the site and appeals: 'Haro, Haro, Haro, à l'aide, mon prince, on me fait tort.' After the Lord's Prayer is said in French the other party is legally bound to halt the disputed act. The effect is identical to an immediate injunction and the case is referred automatically to the Royal Court.

Some accounts suggest that Haro is a corruption of 'ha, Rou' and as such is a reference to Rollo, the first Duke of Normandy and, in his day, the highest judicial authority in the land. From the mid-17th century use of the Clameur has been restricted to cases of interference with real property.

But although the Clameur is now rarely used, there has been a resurgence of interest in Jèrriais, the Jersey language. Said to have developed from one of the Gallo-Roman dialects brought to the Island in the pre-Norman Conquest era, it shares the same origins as the language of William the Conqueror.

The language – purists wince when it is incorrectly described as a patois – was the mother tongue of virtually all Islanders for about a thousand years but its decline accelerated in the post-German Occupation years when increasing anglicisation was coupled with greater access to the influence of the mass media.

Nevertheless, estimates suggest that there are between 7,000 and 10,000 speakers, although proficiency varies. The dialect varies also, with differences being found in the vocabulary between the language spoken in St Ouen and that in St Martin.

The resurgence in interest is apparent in all age groups, with adults enrolling in evening classes and children as young as eight taking lessons in school.

A crown 'peculiar' and 'good' King John

Jersey became part of the Duchy in 933, when it was formally added by Duke William I and it remained so until 1204 when King John was driven from mainland Normandy by the French. Thus, it was part of the Normandy ruled in 1066 by William the Bastard, later the Conqueror and, following victory at Hastings that year, King William I of England. This provides the basis for the claim that the Channel Islands are the Crown's oldest possession. It is this constitutional relationship – that of being a peculiar of the Crown – which prevails today.

The Normans were great church builders and all 12 parish churches existed in the 11th century, although little remains of the originals. Much of the land was then administered by French abbeys but the only one actually built was constructed on L'Islet, the scene of Helier's murder centuries earlier and now the site of Elizabeth Castle.

Following surrender to the French in Rouen in 1204, John lost Normandy. It is from then that Jersey's fiscal independence and constitutional relationship with England is said to have started, although Islanders would suggest 1066 as 'when we conquered England'.

Although much maligned, John has been long regarded as Jersey's great benefactor. The 17th-century historian Philippe Falle wrote: 'No sooner was he apprised of the hazards the Island ran of being overpowered, he, not thinking it enough to send over the necessary succours, hastened himself in person to animate the people and keep up their courage by his presence. He instituted a Royal Court... and gave us a body of Constitutions which have been the foundation of all our franchises to this day, and may not improperly be called our Magna Carta.'

While later authorities cast doubt on the King's visit, and upon some of the constitutions, it is clear that the start of a form of insular government emanated from these times and the Jurats, who still constitute the lay members of the Royal Court – being judges of fact in civil cases and determiners of sentence in criminal ones – and who until 1948 sat also in the States, came into prominence.

But Jersey no longer sat comfortably in the middle of the Crown's land between England and Normandy. It was the closest of the King's possessions to France – just 14 miles away – and defence was necessary. Thus was constructed the magnificent Mont Orgueil (Mount Pride) at Gorey.

The invasion threat remained for centuries and Jersey's coastline retains the evidence – the two principal castles, Martello towers, and St Catherine's Breakwater, built in the mid-19th century and intended to link to a similar but unfinished structure nearby.

Elizabeth Castle, at West Park, was named after Queen Elizabeth I and took nearly half a century to construct. Building started in 1550 and was completed in 1601. Its most famous visitor was the Prince of Wales, later Charles II, who arrived in Jersey in 1646 having fled the Parliamentarian forces in England. After his father was beheaded on 30 January 1649 the new Charles was proclaimed King on 17 February, first on Saturday in the Market Place in St Helier, then the following day at Elizabeth Castle. The castle is also home to the hermitage of St Helier, the patron saint of the Island's capital. Accessible on foot only at low tide, the castle is one of Jersey's foremost historic sites.

Following pages

Ouaisné Bay (pronounced Way-nay) is just one example of the many sandy bays around Jersey's coastline.

Invasion – the constant threat from France

It is from John's time that many of Jersey's ancient offices can be traced. Despite the constant threat from the French, the 13th and 14th centuries saw the administration develop. Originally, responsibility for government was in the hands of a Lord or Warden of the Isles but later the official who presided over the monarch's Court became known as the Bailiff.

Henry III succeeded John and fishing became the Island's chief industry. In pre-Reformation days, with the association of fasting with the Catholic faith, the demand was considerable. The only commodity which Jersey could export on a large scale, it heralded the birth of a commercial association with the sea which has played a significant part in Island life ever since.

The Hundred Years' War followed. Although not a century of uninterrupted fighting between England and France, it meant there was a constant threat of attack and occupation, sometimes for years on end. Jersey was paying dearly for her allegiance to the Crown. But the allegiance held firm and when Henry IV seized the throne he at once renewed the charters confirming all ancient rights and privileges.

Henry V's reign heralded an age of relative stability and prosperity. His seizure of Normandy and subsequent entry into Paris meant Jersey was no longer an outpost and the front line was far from its shores.

But the fragile hold on stability was not to last. Henry V and his father-in-law, who theoretically ruled France, died in 1422. The infant Henry VI became sovereign of both nations. Seven years later Joan of Arc appeared at the head of the French forces. Without her, Jersey's subsequent history would have changed dramatically for, albeit inadvertently, she saved the Channel Islands from becoming part of France.

Had Henry V's vision of uniting the nations become reality, the wealthier French would have become the dominant partner, government would have been centred in Paris, not London, subsequent monarchs would have been more French than English, and England relegated to an outlying province. French-speaking Jersey, just 14 miles from mainland Normandy, would certainly have become French.

England may well have won the battle with St Joan, and burned her at the stake, but towards the end of the conflict they lost command of the sea and by the middle of the 15th century, one of the Wardens had to pay a French admiral in order to cross the Channel safely.

Government develops and so does a fishing fleet

Further periods of occupation followed, as the French took advantage of the War of the Roses.

When Henry VII succeeded towards the end of the 15th century the name 'Etats' was probably already being used to describe the government Assembly. In 1497, for example, the security of the endowments for two schools was guaranteed by 'the consent of all the States' (les Etats). The earliest recorded Act of the States is dated 1524.

As one historian wrote, as Jersey emerged slowly from medievalism, the important buildings were the churches, mills and castles, serving soul, body and defence. All were built of granite but there were probably no really impressive manor houses, except perhaps St Ouen's, until well into the 17th century.

The Elizabethan age saw the further development of two industries which were to become pillars of the economy. By the end of the 16th century documentary reference was being made to trade with Newfoundland. Jerseymen were sailing the Atlantic in spring and returning in autumn to plough the land.

By the early 1600s the fishing fleet was so crucial to the economy that St Brelade was permitted to hold its spring Communion earlier than other churches so that its fishermen might become communicants before sailing.

At about the same time knitting also came to the fore. Mary, Queen of Scots, was led to her execution wearing, among other things, 'next to her leggs a pair of Jersey hose white…'

Documents from Elizabethan days refer to the extent of sheep rearing, with the demand for wool so great that imports were necessary. Knitting was so profitable that men took it up and the States became worried that this would adversely affect farming. In 1608 it was decreed that 'during the harvest and vraicing season all persons shall stop making stockings and work on the land on pain of imprisonment on bread and water and the confiscation of their work'. 'Vraicing' refers to vraic, the name still used for seaweed gathered from the beaches, heaped in stacks and used on the land as fertiliser. The practice continues, although not to the extent that it did until the early 1960s.

In 1600 Sir Walter Raleigh was appointed Governor, probably the most distinguished ever to have held the post, but Jersey saw little of him. However, he was present in the States in 1602 when the establishment of a land registry was approved.

Since then, and perhaps for some time before, all contracts involving land purchase and the buildings constructed on it, along with documentation relating to inherited real property, have been registered by the Royal Court.

Even today, parties involved in the sale and purchase of a house have to appear before the Royal Court to raise a gloveless right hand and swear 'upon pain of perjury' to abide by the contract – a more significant event in a family's life than simply exchanging documents in a lawyer's office.

Raleigh also saved the magnificent Mont Orgueil from destruction. His predecessor, Sir Anthony Poulet, had decided that the considerable amount of money spent on the castle by his father and grandfather had been wasted and a new structure was needed.

Work began towards the end of the 16th century on the islet of St Helier but when Raleigh took office he decided that both fortresses were needed. It was Raleigh who named the new castle after his sovereign, the now ageing Queen Elizabeth, saying that he 'presumed to christen it Fort Isabella Bellissima' – Elizabeth Castle the most beautiful.

A view of **St Helier** which illustrates the massive expansion and change that the town has undergone. From the broad sweep of Almorah Crescent, a fine example of Regency architecture, in the background, down to the high-rise flats at Hue Court in the centre of town and the granite warehouses, now home to the Maritime Museum, that border the Old Harbour.

Following pages

St Ouen's Bay, the longest stretch of white sand in the Island and a surfer's paradise, with Corbière Lighthouse in the distance.

The King or Parliament?

Jersey wanted no part in the English Civil War but it became embroiled and the conflict left a significant mark on its history. From the start, Jersey appeared to support the King, Charles I, with Guernsey supporting Parliament. Whether the legacy of this is associated with Guernsey not using the Sovereign's effigy on the obverse of coins until recently is questionable, but it is a continuing argument in rivalry between the two islands.

The reasons had little to do with the dispute. Guernsey's main reason for supporting Parliament was religious. The King, with his belief in the Divine Right and French Catholic wife, had little appeal for Calvinistic Guernseymen.

For Jersey's part, divisions centred on support or otherwise for Royalist Sir Philip de Carteret, as Bailiff and Lieut-Governor the most powerful man in the Island, and later his son-in-law Captain George Carteret. Without them, the majority of ordinary folk would have supported Parliament, for they too had strong Calvinistic leanings.

When Sir Philip died in 1643, Charles appointed Captain Carteret to succeed him. Parliament supporters who had gained control prior to his arrival fled, no resistance was offered when he came to Jersey, and Carteret was sworn in at Trinity Church.

In 1646 the Prince of Wales, later Charles II, arrived in Jersey with an entourage, most of whom stayed with him at Elizabeth Castle. Having fled Cromwell's forces in England, he was grateful for a warm welcome and stayed several months.

His father was beheaded on 30 January 1649 and on 17 February Charles was proclaimed King. The proclamation was then nailed to the door of the Royal Court House. The original document, written in French, was saved and is now in the Jersey Museum. It bears the signatures of 26 men; brave men, given that they had denounced the beheading of Charles I as a 'horrible outrage' and England was controlled by Parliamentarians.

Thus the reign of Charles II began in Jersey in 1649 and not, as elsewhere, in 1660.

The original seal, which was granted to the Bailiwick of Jersey in 1279 by King Edward I.

Many new public buildings were erected at the latter end of the 19th century, including the **States Chamber** in the Royal Square in 1887. The chair on the right, occupied by the Bailiff of Jersey, is seven inches higher than that on the left, occupied by the Lieut-Governor. This signifies the Island's autonomy in its internal affairs.

Colombiers and colonies

Charles II was in Holland when his father was beheaded but when the Dutch suggested his continued presence was 'inconvenient' he joined his mother in Paris. However, his 'absence was impatiently desired' by the French and Jersey provided the only place of refuge.

Stories of the houses in which he is purported to have stayed still exist today, but are probably false. The contemporary testimony of the diarist Jean Chevalier makes clear that if any of the gentry invited the King to their house, the invitation was declined, Lords of the Court attending instead, something the King took as a compliment.

What the historian Balleine described as the King's 'easy-going amiability' made him popular. Laurens Hamptonne was allowed to rebuild a dovecot, thus elevating his house to the rank of manor. That might not be worth mentioning were it not for the fact that the property, Hamptonne in St Lawrence, was bought with help from the States by the National Trust for Jersey in 1987. The property, including the 17th-century garden and the colombier (the dovecot), has since been renovated and is a Country Life Museum.

Charles left in February 1650. His departure led to attempts by Cromwell to recapture Jersey and in December 1651 the garrison at Elizabeth Castle surrendered. Carteret secured extraordinarily favourable conditions for himself and later joined the French navy, becoming a Vice-Admiral.

Charles II was left a vagabond king without a kingdom. That situation existed until after Oliver Cromwell's death but on 2 June 1660, four weeks after Charles II had been proclaimed King in London, he was again proclaimed King in Jersey.

The Royalists soon reaped their rewards. Sir George Carteret was given manors in Cornwall and Devon, made one of eight proprietors of Carolina and, in March 1664, he received another province in America which still bears the name he gave it – New Jersey.

However, of more significance to Jersey, Charles presented the Island with a huge silver-gilt mace 'to be carried before the Bailiffs in perpetual memory of their fidelity to his august father and himself'.

That same mace is still carried before the Bailiff on all official occasions and placed before his chair in the Royal Court and the States Chamber – a practice which even the German Occupation did not halt. On the death of the Sovereign it is draped in black chiffon and laid flat on the table. This, according to Balleine, recognises the superiority of the spiritual over the temporal power and is one of the few occasions on which the mace does not remain upright.

The inscription is a proud reminder to Jerseymen of their loyalty to their Sovereign: *Tali haud omnes dignatur honore* – Not all doth he deem worthy of such an honour.

This silver-gilt mace, pictured in the States Chamber, was presented to the Island by King Charles II in recognition of Jersey's loyalty to both him and his father, King Charles I. It is still carried before the Bailiff on all official occasions and placed before his chair in the Royal Court and the States Chamber.

Historians, cider making and books

Charles II was succeeded by his brother, James II, a Roman Catholic who sought to re-establish that faith. When news of William of Orange's landing in England in 1688 reached Jersey, sighs of relief greeted the prospect of being free of French influence and Popery.

A year later England and France were at war again and Islanders resumed privateering, having during the Civil War become known as the scourge of the Channel.

But less glamorous forms of livelihood were also pursued, notably agriculture, knitting, cider making and fishing. However, the Civil War had had its effect on trade and contemporary accounts refer to poverty in Jersey.

Many emigrated to new lives across the Atlantic, far from the feudalism still prevalent at the start of the 18th century. But those who remained were becoming more erudite and the end of the 17th century saw the publication of three descriptive accounts of Jersey, all written by Jerseymen – Jurat Jean Poingdestre, Philippe Dumaresq and the Rev Philippe Falle.

They wrote of the changing face of Jersey over the previous century. Falle estimated the population to be somewhere between fifteen and twenty thousand. A hundred years earlier, Jersey had been an island of open fields, with hedges almost unknown. While crops were in the ground even pigs were tethered. At this time, a large part of the Island was covered in orchards and both Falle and Poingdestre wrote of the advent of enclosing land to make fields.

However, said Falle, they were not fences as in England but 'great bulwarks of earth' crowned with a hedge of whitethorn. Between were narrow lanes, heavily shaded by overhanging trees and controlled, as they are today, by a mandatory twice-yearly branchage policed by the 12 parish authorities. Owners or occupiers of land are required to cut back all hedges and overhanging branches bordering public roads. Those not complying are fined and ordered to do the work.

The chroniclers all deplored the demise in agriculture. Hitherto, sufficient corn had been grown to feed the residents with enough left over for export but towards the end of the 17th century it became necessary to import. One reason was the huge increase in cider making, caused no doubt by a change in drinking habits, and Poingdestre remarked that Jersey was in danger of 'becoming a continual orchard'.

Falle later moved to England and in 1729 gave the States part of his collection of books, some two thousand volumes, to start a public library, along with £300 towards the cost of a suitable building. The original building still stands in the appropriately named Library Place, a few yards from the Royal Square.

Commercial activity increased and with it the development of the town. A corn market was built in 1669 by Suzanne Dumaresq in exchange for permission to build a dwelling above it. Those buildings now face the Royal Square and are respectively the Office of the Superintendent Registrar and the United Club.

At the other end is the statue of King George II, unveiled in 1751. The Market Place was renamed the Royal Square in his honour, although for many years it continued to be called le marchi or le vier marchi. Nearby is the Chamber of Commerce, founded in February 1768 and the oldest in the English-speaking world.

The following year was marked by civil unrest, with accounts describing 'great disturbances' over the export of corn. In September 1769 men of the northern parishes of St Martin, St John and Trinity marched to town. They forced their way into the Court House, where the Assise d'Heritage was sitting, and threatened the Court for several hours.

It is worth recording that the Assise, said to be the oldest land Court in Europe, still exists. The seigneurs of the now ceremonial fiefs answer when called, while advocates of the Royal Court renew their oaths. When the monarch attends, the seigneurs pay homage and traditional customs, such as the presentation of two mallards on a silver dish by the Seigneur of Trinity, and the function of the Seigneur of Rosel as the hereditary butler to the Duke of Normandy, are maintained.

The riot was a manifestation of discontent and led to instructions from England that reforms be introduced. By Order in Council, the Royal Court was stripped of its power to legislate and became simply a court. Legislation was also consolidated into what became known as the Code of 1771 and parts remained in force for almost 200 years.

The final repeal removed the maximum five per cent limit on interest rates and gave birth to Jersey's finance industry.

A legacy of the **German Occupation** of the Island during the Second World War can be seen on many coasts and headlands. Hitler had decreed that Jersey should be an impregnable fortress so huge concrete fortifications were constructed at many key points around the Island, usually by slave labour.

The Battle of Jersey – the French invade!

In 1776, France began to send arms and money to help Americans in their War of Independence. Once more Jersey faced the threat of invasion.

England's response was to allow Jersey to resume privateering against French shipping becoming, according to one French general, 'the despair of France'. A number of invasion attempts were made and these culminated in what became known as the Battle of Jersey.

Commanding the French force was Baron de Rullecourt, who sailed from Granville on 27 December 1780 with almost a thousand men. But the wind was against him and it was not until 5 January that it turned.

He landed at La Rocque, a moonscape at low tide of jagged rocks stretching two miles out to sea and an unlikely invasion site. Guided by a local man who had fled to escape hanging, de Rullecourt's 26 vessels sailed up a narrow passage at midnight. The militiamen were celebrating Twelfth Night. The invasion went undetected.

Leaving a hundred men at La Rocque, de Rullecourt marched with six hundred others into town, arriving just before sunrise on 6 January 1781. The Lieut-Governor, Major Moyse Corbet, was in bed when news of the invasion reached him. Escape was impossible – the French were at his door. Told by de Rullecourt that the six hundred were only an advance guard and another four thousand had occupied strategic points around the Island, while a further ten thousand would land before nightfall, Corbet decided resistance was futile and signed a surrender document.

But elsewhere, others reached a different decision. Captain Aylward, commanding troops at Elizabeth Castle, ignored the order and his men opened fire when the French tried to cross the causeway. Captain Mulcaster, in a typically British gesture, returned the surrender demand, saying he did not understand French.

Several miles away in St Peter was a 24-year-old major, Francis Peirson, temporarily commanding the 95th Foot while more senior officers were on Christmas leave. Hearing of the French landing, he and his men marched to Gallows Hill – now Westmount – to join Highlanders and the Jersey Militia in a force of some 1,600.

But the young Yorkshireman was in a difficult position when Corbet's order to surrender arrived. Could he disobey his commander, the Lieut-Governor?

Peirson dispatched his adjutant under a flag of truce to establish if Corbet had signed under duress. De Rullecourt responded by sending Corbet to see Peirson and demand obedience but the latter told him that he and his forces preferred death to surrender and gave him ten minutes to get back to the centre of town.

With French troops concentrated in the Royal Square, Peirson sent part of his force to seize the Town Hill, where Fort Regent now stands. From there they had an unobstructed line of fire into the Square. He sent his main force up what is now Broad Street while he led another party up what is now part of the King Street pedestrian precinct, entering the Royal Square through the cutting now called Peirson Place, adjacent to the public house named after the gallant major.

Hopelessly outnumbered, the French lasted less than ten minutes before surrendering, but by this time both de Rullecourt and Peirson were dead.

As the historian Balleine has recorded, a simple stone in St Helier's churchyard bears the name de Rullecourt but the site of his grave is unknown. Within the church there is a memorial to Peirson and, near the chancel step, a gravestone inscribed with the one word 'Peirson' – 'a silent and eloquent testimony to this very brave young Englishman who earned the undying gratitude of Jersey'.

The battle was also commemorated in the magnificent Death of Major Peirson, by John Singleton Copley. When the original was offered for sale by Copley's son, the States tried to buy it but were outbid and the painting is now in the collection of the Tate Gallery, London. A copy by the artist Holyoake, commissioned by the States, hangs in the Royal Court.

Moyse Corbet later faced a court martial where, although his defence that he knew his officers would disobey his orders and his actions had saved the town and given British units time to assemble was largely accepted, he was stripped of his Lieut-Governorship but retained his pension.

Never again was Jersey to be attacked by the French. The next invasion, over 150 years later, was to be from a new enemy and was altogether swifter, more successful and lead to five long years of occupation.

Jersey's historic **Royal Square** in **St Helier**, the scene of the Battle of Jersey in 1781.

One of the entrances to the **Royal Square**.

A gilded statue of **King George II** dressed as Julius Caesar stands in the Royal Square in St Helier.

Politics and election mischief

Internal politics replaced the threat from the French with the emergence of two political groups, the Charlots and the Magots, later the Laurel and the Rose parties. They were born of the unrest caused when the States tried to regulate currency used in the Island in the 1730s.

The parties manifested themselves 40 years later with a challenge to the power of the Lemprière family. The States played second fiddle to the Royal Court and when Charles Lemprière was Lieut-Bailiff – the Bailiff was Earl Granville, who never visited Jersey – his father, father-in-law, a cousin and two brothers-in-law all held office as Jurat, and the Jurats were only twelve in number. In 1758 Lemprière's brother

Philippe became Attorney-General. The power bloc was virtually complete.

Despite the introduction of the Code of 1771 and other reforms forced on Charles Lemprière, he remained powerful, but opposition led by a liberal young lawyer, Jean Dumaresq, was increasing.

Elections for offices such as parish Constable and Jurat became ferocious affairs. Neither political party hesitated to break the law. Bribery, corruption and even the kidnapping of voters were all commonplace. Stories handed down for generations tell of electors being seized and taken to the Ecréhous on polling day, while others were plied with drink, rendering them incapable of voting.

By the Battle of Jersey in 1781, Dumaresq and the Magots had a majority in the States and were heading towards a similar situation among the Jurats. But that majority was often rendered ineffective because Lemprière would leave the chair, effectively closing the States sitting, whenever he disagreed with propositions.

The Island issues its own banknotes and coinage.

This stamp, issued to mark the Millennium on 1st January 2000, includes 22 carat gold hot metallic stamping and embossing in its design. It features the **Crest of Jersey**, the three leopards, originally the armorial bearings of Richard I.

Despite all this, commercial life continued. Trade with Newfoundland and its fishing industry led to the development of boatyards and there are reminders today at Gorey, Havre des Pas and the Waterfront of their importance. Oyster fishing was another developing industry. An oyster bed had always existed off Gorey – early in the 17th century the Governor had claimed it as Crown property, only for the Royal Court to overrule him, declaring that every Jerseyman had the right to fish there.

For many years the industry was confined to local fishermen but early in the 19th century it attracted outside attention. Upwards of 2,000 men were eventually employed – the average catch per day was 12,000 oysters per boat and there were about three hundred vessels – and hundreds of women worked in packing sheds.

To accommodate this burgeoning immigrant population, rows of cottages were built at Gorey – the picturesque village in the shadow of Mont Orgueil and overlooking the Royal Bay of Grouville.

Jersey took over control of the Post Office from the British Government in 1969. Demand for local stamps is still considerable.

Cows and potatoes – Jersey's gold mines

Late in the 18th century the States approved an Act which, although never intended, led to the development of the famous Jersey breed of cattle – renowned the world over for its milk's high butterfat content.

At that time cattle from Jersey could be exported to England without hindrance but there was a substantial import duty on those exported from France. Shrewd Normandy farmers realised that by using Jersey as a staging post and leaving their animals to graze for a week, they could avoid import duty and export freely to England.

This led to a glut and the price of livestock fell. The States took action, imposing a substantial fine for each animal landed, along with forfeiture of the vessel bringing it and the slaughter of the beast.

Until then, cattle in Jersey had been developed from various strains of the commonplace breeds elsewhere. However, this 1789 Act prohibited the importation of live animals and Jersey developed the breed which is characteristically its own, although it was to take a further half century for the animal we know today to emerge. By 1860 it was reported that over 1,100 cows had been exported to England at an average price of £16 a head. Within 20 years prices up to £400 an animal were not rare and American buyers were paying up to £1,000 for a single animal.

A century later what the historian Balleine described as 'another gold mine' was discovered. A farmer, Hugh de la Haye, had been the recipient of the old custom of the Big Plough (la Grand-'tchéthue in Jèrriais), where farmers brought horses to help neighbours plough.

Hosting the traditional supper, de la Haye passed around two large potatoes given him by a local store. These were cut into pieces – one had 16 eyes – and planted the following day. In spring they produced a large and exceptionally early crop and, unlike their round parents, the new potatoes were kidney shaped.

De la Haye nurtured his new crop carefully until he had enough to trade with and then exhibited his produce in the window of the newspaper, *La Nouvelle Chronique*, whose owner, Charles Le Feuvre, named the variety the Royal Jersey Fluke.

The total export in 1891 of what is now an appellation-protected crop called the Jersey Royal amounted to 70,000 tons, worth nearly half a million pounds. Little wonder Balleine described it as a gold mine.

Victoria and the birth of democracy

Victorian times brought a Royal Visit when the young Queen came, albeit for only three hours, in 1846. Although Charles II had visited as a fugitive, this was the first recorded state visit and the public demanded a permanent reminder.

In May 1850 the foundation stone of Victoria College was laid, with the opening two years later. Other marks of loyalty were to follow. In 1890 her statue, now at West Park, was unveiled at the Weighbridge, her diamond jubilee saw the founding of the Victoria Cottage Homes for the elderly at St Saviour and the same year Victoria Avenue, now a dual carriageway providing the main route between St Helier and the west, was named.

However, Royal visits or not, the political battles continued. The Laurel and Rose parties had by then developed and in the 1850s the former was in control, refusing to sanction even modest reforms.

But the Privy Council – the body which, rather than the British Government, has responsibility for Jersey's good governance – finally lost patience and issued Orders in Council establishing Police (Magistrate) and Petty Debts courts and a professional police force.

A clear violation of Jersey's right to enact its own legislation, it aroused furious protest. The Royal Court refused to register the Orders but, after almost two years of negotiation, a compromise was reached. The Orders were revoked by the Privy Council and the States approved virtually all the original provisions.

However, there was a more far-reaching consequence. The States realised that further reform was necessary. Clearly, if Jersey was to remain responsible for its internal affairs, the Assembly – which had hitherto consisted of Jurats elected for life, the 12 parish Rectors who sat until their incumbency ended and the Constables, who although not elected directly to the House sat, as they do today, by virtue of their office – would have to become more democratic by including people elected directly.

Thus the office of Deputy was established and in 1857 elections for 14 were held, one for each country parish and three for St Helier. But it was to be almost a century – the post-war reforms of 1948 – before voters became entitled to elect every representative.

Those reforms led to the present constitution of an Assembly which now comprises 12 Senators, elected on an all-Island basis for six-year terms, 29 Deputies, who are voted in by either whole parishes or on a constituency basis, and the 12 Constables. Government is by committees made up of a president and up to six others, although changes to a ministerial system have been proposed and are currently being debated.

The 20th century – golf, theatre & the benefactors

When Victoria came to the throne in 1837, the population numbered about 36,000, with most speaking Jersey Norman French. However, as the 20th century dawned the population had grown by almost half as much again and English was gradually increasing in usage. In 1901, amid furious opposition, the use of English was made optional in the States, although Members still answer the roll call in French and votes are taken as 'pour' and 'contre' – for or against.

The new century saw also the creation of many institutions, some of which remain, notably the annual Battle of Flowers, held on the second Thursday in August, which in 2002 celebrated its centenary.

The recently-renovated Opera House opened originally in 1900 with a production starring one of Jersey's most famous daughters, Lillie Langtry. Emily Le Breton, the daughter of the Rector of St Saviour who later became Dean of Jersey, was famously the mistress of Edward VII. She is buried in St Saviour's churchyard.

In 1924 the States agreed to admit women to the Assembly, although the first was not elected for another 20 years and it would be many decades before the first woman Constable, Iris Le Feuvre, took her seat.

Income Tax was introduced in 1928 with the stipulation that it should not be more than a shilling in the pound. Only during the German Occupation did it rise to four shillings (20p), at which figure it remains today.

And, as they had done for centuries, Jerseymen were still making their mark in the rest of the world, notably the golfers Harry Vardon and Ted Ray. Vardon won the British Open Championship on six occasions and both men also won the US Open – for many years the only Britons to have done so.

There were benefactors too, perhaps the best known being T B Davis, a Jerseyman who had made a fortune in South Africa. Between the wars he made substantial gifts, notably the magnificent Howard Davis Park, the States Experimental Farm at Trinity, the Howard Hall at Victoria College, and the Howard Davis lifeboat, all of which were given in memory of his son, Howard Leopold Davis, who died in the Great War.

Davis's yacht *Westward* was scuttled on his instructions on his death but its mainmast was saved and is now the flagstaff at Howard Davis Park. The site of the park had been owned by Davis's former employer and the young man vowed on leaving his job that he would return, buy the property, raze the house to the ground and create a park. He did so.

Other benefactors of the time included Sir Jesse Boot, later Lord Trent, whose wife was Jersey-born Florence Rowe. Their legacy includes the FB Playing Fields and St Matthew's Church at Millbrook, familiarly known as the Glass Church because of its magnificent Lalique glass fittings.

But the 'between the wars' prosperity, which had provided considerable income from agriculture and a developing tourism industry, as well as the first wealthy immigrants attracted by low taxes, was about to halt, albeit temporarily.

Green Street Cemetery in the foreground provides a haven of peace amongst the burgeoning development in St Helier. The row of red brick offices, centre right, was built on the site of the Forum Cinema. They now house the offices of some of the biggest names in international finance.

The Occupation – Jersey under the jackboot

War broke out in September 1939. By June 1940 France had fallen and was occupied. It was inevitable that the Channel Islands would suffer the same fate.

On 27 June German planes were over Jersey. Despite the islands having been declared a demilitarised zone, machine gunning and bombs dropping started the following day. A number of civilians were killed and injured.

On 1 July a lone German aircraft landed at the Airport. The Bailiff, Alexander Coutanche, who had earlier lowered the Union Flag at Fort Regent, had no option but to hand over the Island to the enemy. Jersey would be under the jackboot for the next five years.

The Germans settled in. At one time there were as many as 16,000 occupying troops and the figure rarely fell below 10,000.

In October 1941 Hitler, fearing a British invasion, ordered that Jersey be made an impregnable fortress. Slave labour from Occupied Europe poured in and the coastline became a mass of concrete and steel. While the barbed wire has largely disappeared, Jersey remains studded with grim concrete reminders of five of the darkest years in its history.

A huge underground hospital, now a museum, was built in St Peter's Valley. Wireless sets were banned in June 1942 and over 10,000 handed in, although many were ingeniously hidden. Even then, over 700 sets were discovered during the Occupation and their owners jailed. Indeed, so frequent were prosecutions that after sentencing the 'criminals' returned home until the prison could accommodate them.

But if the ban on listening to the BBC aroused the muted anger of the population, worse followed. In September 1942, again on the express orders of Hitler, all non-native residents, along with their families, were told to present themselves for deportation and subsequent internment in Germany.

It was an act which caused distress and indignation and although deportees were not badly treated, some died during internment. However, in a gesture of reconciliation instigated primarily by ex-internees, parishioners of St Helier in 2002 agreed to twin with Bad Wurzach, the village site of one such camp.

Meanwhile, food and other essential commodities became scarcer. Sea water was boiled for salt, an estimated quarter of a million trees were felled for fuel, wood and pieces of tyre rubber were used to make and repair footwear, and those rations which were available eventually petered out. The situation worsened after D-Day as virtually all transport links with mainland Europe ceased.

Thousands were saved from starvation only by the arrival at the end of 1944 of the Red Cross ship *Vega*. The letters of the vessel's name can be found in the Royal Square, the 'V' placed in the form of granite paving by a stonemason who carried out his work under the noses of the Germans.

8 May 1945 was VE-Day and in his victory broadcast, Prime Minister Winston Churchill declared that 'Our dear Channel Islands are to be freed today'. His speech was relayed to huge crowds in the Royal Square and the following day, to incredibly joyous scenes, British troops arrived on *HMS Beagle*.

The Occupation was over and 9 May – Liberation Day – has been celebrated as a public holiday ever since.

During the German Occupation, **V for Victory signs** began to appear all over Jersey, painted by Islanders keen to show their resistance to the Germans. This resulted in severe punishment for those who were discovered. But one V, etched in granite by a brave stonemason as he repaved the Royal Square, remained unnoticed by the occupying forces.

At street level many **St Helier** shop fronts have lost the character of the era in which they were built. One exception is the Central Market in Halkett Place and Beresford Street.

Post-war recovery – the finance industry arrives

Jersey's recovery has been little short of astonishing. A community left on the point of starvation in 1945 is now one of the world's most affluent.

But there has been a price. The post-war tourism boom coincided with development on an unprecedented scale. Residential qualifications were introduced because Jersey became so popular that the indigenous population had difficulty in affording homes.

Land, especially that for development, was at a premium but, thanks to a succession of planning authorities, the unsightly ribbon development which has spoiled the Guernsey countryside has been largely avoided.

However, while St Peter Port has retained much of its 'gateway to Guernsey' charm, the same cannot be said of the approach to St Helier from the sea, although that may improve as the Waterfront development started at the end of the 20th century takes shape.

But the most far-reaching impact on the lives of residents has been that of the finance industry. Until the early 1970s, the two principal pillars of Jersey's economy were tourism and agriculture. The abolition of the five per cent limit on interest payments heralded an influx of banks from all over the world.

The industry has since broadened its base and while international banks are still anxious to do business in Jersey, other facets of finance have been introduced. Bank deposits held in the Island in mid-2002 stood at £136 billion, the value of collective investment funds at the same time was £107 billion, while monies in investment management schemes totalled £31 billion.

The benefits have been enormous, with huge investment in health, education and social services. But the expansion of the banks, trust companies and the law and accountancy firms needed to service the industry resulted in massive pressure on housing and labour markets.

Jersey's relationship with the European community, negotiated in the 1970s, means the Island is not part of the European Union, and neither pays VAT nor has direct representation in Brussels, but has retained its traditional tariff-free trading relationship with the UK – and with it the extended European market.

Sadly, international competition in the historic primary industries of agriculture and tourism has led to a contraction of both and, with signs that the years of rapid growth in the finance industry may be nearing a plateau, many believe that there may be at least one or two clouds appearing in a hitherto sunny sky.

However, there is little doubt that Jersey, with its ancient traditions of adaptability and stubbornness, will meet and overcome any challenge the 21st century may bring, just as it has since man first set foot on its productive soil.

Office accommodation in **St Helier** illustrates the changing face of architecture over the last 100 years

Opposite
The **Jersey Sculpture Trust** has been responsible for the erection of several sculptures like this one at the top of Queen Street, which leads down to King Street and forms the backbone of St Helier's main shopping precinct.

The **King Street** precinct decorated for the festive period.

Not quite Oxford Street, but St Helier sparkles in the run-up to Christmas.

Although shipping costs can affect the prices charged in Jersey shops, shoppers still look for VAT-free bargains.

Built to celebrate the centenary of the Battle of Jersey, the **Central Market** in **St Helier** is a fine example of a Victorian covered market. Its centrepiece is a 15-ft tiered fountain and its ornate roof is reminiscent of a 19th-century English railway station. Although many of the traditional greengrocery and butchers' stalls have disappeared, a few remain. They have been joined by small cafés and enclosed shops selling a variety of specialist goods.

A look to first-floor level while walking through St Helier will reveal much of the original architecture as well as interesting features such as Britannia, above the **Lamplighter public house** in Mulcaster Street.

The façade of the **Mechanics Institute** in Halkett Place. Now a working men's club with a strong tradition of billiards and snooker, the building was in use as a post office between 1881-1909.

There is a strong history of Methodism in Jersey dating back to the late 18th century. A large number of Methodist churches were built during the following 100 years. Many are still in use but several have either been demolished or are used for other purposes. The most imposing is **Wesley Grove** at the northern end of Halkett Place, built in 1847 and named after Methodism's founder John Wesley.

The **Opera House** in Gloucester Street, opened in 1900, was extensively refurbished in time for its centenary, as one of the Island's Millennium projects.

Opposite
Tile and slate roofs and tiny buildings have made way for the large, flat blocks that house Jersey's flourishing **finance sector**.

Following pages
The horseshoe-shaped auditorium of the **Opera House** is a fine example of an Edwardian theatre. The building opened in 1900 with a production starring Lillie Langtry. Lillie was born Emily Le Breton, the daughter of the then Rector of St Saviour who later became Dean of Jersey, and she was famously the mistress of King Edward VII.

In the **Town Church** is this simple memorial to Major Francis Peirson, the brave soldier who died at the moment of victory against French invaders in the Battle of Jersey in 1781.

Constructed in the 1880s of pink Jersey granite and grey granite from Brittany, the Gothic-style **St Thomas's Church** at the junction of Val Plaisant and Victoria Street is hailed as the finest Roman Catholic church in Jersey. The cross on its spire stands 196 feet above the ground and is a town landmark.

Named after the Queen, **Victoria College** was opened in 1852.

The statue in the foreground was erected to the memory of **Lieutenant-General Sir George Don**, who was Lieut-Governor of Jersey from 1806-1814. During his time in the Island he did so much to improve the roads that a road, a street and a bridge were named after him. Beyond the statue of Don is the Island's Cenotaph and to the left of the park is Cyril Le Marquand House, which houses several States departments and was named after a Senator who, as President of the Finance and Economics Committee, is credited as the architect of the finance industry.

Opposite page
A corner of **Howard Davis Park**, where the bodies of allied servicemen washed up in the Island during the German Occupation were originally interred. The most recent burial, however, was that of a Jerseyman, Maurice Gould, whose remains were returned to his native island in the 1990s from Germany where he died during the war.

The theme 'floral island' was originally developed as part of a tourism campaign. The idea has held true, however, and in spring and summer Jersey is ablaze with colour.

Until a few years ago daffodil and bulb production was a major source of income for Jersey growers. Competition has all but decimated the industry so while fields of blooming daffodils may look pretty, it actually means that they have been left to flower because prices were too low to make export viable.

One of many navigation aids around the coast. This imposing structure is at **Grève d'Azette**.

Opposite page and below
The seawater bathing pool at **Havre des Pas** was originally opened in 1895. It was renovated as a Millennium project.

The Old Harbour in St Helier is used primarily for the berthing of locally-owned boats.

Recent land reclamation around the Island's waterfront has provided opportunities to develop attractive walks adjacent to the sea.

Leaving St Helier Harbour with **Elizabeth Castle** in the background, this vessel maintains Jersey's centuries-old tradition of sea fishing.

Opposite

As boating becomes an ever more popular pastime, marinas have been incorporated into the redeveloped St Helier waterfront to accommodate sailors from the other Channel Islands, the UK and France as well as local boats.

Ariadne the steam driven clock, designed in the shape of a paddle steamer, is the world's largest steam clock. It was erected as part of an ongoing major investment in St Helier's waterfront adjacent to the Maritime Museum. The clock is driven by a steam engine, the steam for which is generated by an independent electric boiler. There is also a satellite link, which enables the clock to receive a signal from the UK, which corrects any inaccuracies of time to ensure that it is always telling the correct time.

Virtually obsolete, these cranes provide a reminder of the time when all goods coming into and leaving the Island had to be lifted on and off ships. The dome in the background is part of the roof of **Fort Regent Leisure Centre**, formerly an imposing fortification guarding the town and approaches of St Helier.

Emeraude Lines runs a regular car ferry service between Jersey/Guernsey and St Malo.

Condor Ferries provides a year-round ferry service between Jersey and the UK mainland using the new-generation InCat craft.

The distinctive **Commodore Shipping** logo.

Previous pages
The **Commodore Goodwill** leaves St Helier for Portsmouth. The **Condor Express** can also be seen outward bound from the Island for Poole.

The **Commodore Clipper** and **Commodore Goodwill** ferries bring freight to the Island and ship locally-grown produce out. They also provide a valuable alternative to the fastcraft during the winter months when the English Channel proves too rough for the modern ships.

Elizabeth Castle – the gateway to St Helier's harbours.

The imposing **Elizabeth Castle**, which stands on its own islet outside St Helier, is floodlit at night.

St Helier's Hermitage stands on a rock on the breakwater on the south side of Elizabeth Castle. It is believed that the tiny chapel was built by the monks of St Helier's Abbey and that the hermit St Helier lived there for 15 years in the sixth century. The Hermitage can be accessed by way of a narrow flight of stone stairs and is the scene of an annual pilgrimage on St Helier's Day in July.

Although its design was based on the outline of a fish, **La Frégate Café**, built on reclaimed land at the western end of the Esplanade, is referred to locally as 'the upturned boat'. But despite local opprobrium the café, designed by world-famous architect Will Alsop working in partnership with local architects Mason Design Partnership, has received much international acclaim in the architectural press.

The Jersey **Battle of Flowers** celebrated its centenary in 2002. The first 'Battle' was held to celebrate the Coronation of King Edward VII and since then the event, held in August, has developed into a major tourist attraction for the Island. As well as dozens of flower-bedecked floats, work on which starts months before the event, the arena comes alive with dancers, bands and all manner of carnival activity. And the sun always shines... the Jersey Battle of Flowers has never been rained off, despite some close calls.

The interior of **St Matthew's Church** at Millbrook is lavishly decorated with glass by René Lalique of Paris. Known as 'The Glass Church', it was reconstructed in 1934 by Lady Trent, formerly Miss Florence Rowe, in memory of her husband Jesse Boot – the first Baron Trent of Nottingham and the founder of Boots the Chemist.

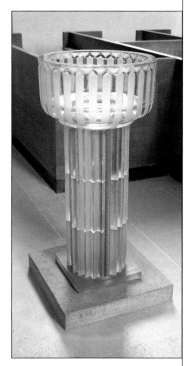

A lily design is one of the many **Lalique glass** features.

The **Lalique** font is believed to be the only glass one in the British Isles.

The **panels** in the entrance doors at St Matthew's are made of Lalique glass, as are many other features in the building

Opposite page
The exterior of **St Mathew's Church** at Millbrook is plain in comparison with the highly decorated interior.

These catamarans are pictured at **St Aubin's Bay**, a popular venue for the sea sports which feature prominently in Jersey's summer calendar.

Every community has its eccentrics. Robert Chalmers Besau's house at **Mont Cochon** has become something of a tourist attraction since he painted religious tracts over it.

The picturesque village and port of **St Aubin** is on the opposite side of St Aubin's Bay to St Helier, three miles away. The harbour, although once a busier port than St Helier, has retained its charm. Steep, narrow streets lead down to the harbour, which houses visiting and local pleasure craft, and restaurants and small shops line the pretty bulwarks.

Opposite page

St Brelade's Parish Hall, which was formerly a railway terminus, is situated alongside the harbour at St Aubin. The area in front has recently been redeveloped into a peaceful seating area.

Following pages

St Aubin at dusk when natural and artificial light combine.

Below

St Aubin's Fort, in St Aubin's Bay, inaccessible at high tide, is used by youth groups as an activity centre.

Noirmont Point is familiar to sea travellers as one of the roughest stretches of water around the Island. The views from the headland are some of the most spectacular in Jersey.

The **Lavender Farm** in **St Brelade** has grown into a significant tourist attraction. More than 90 different species of lavender grow here – one of the largest collections in the British Isles. It's a real working farm with a modern distillery where the lavender is turned into a variety of products.

On the headland at **Noirmont Point** stands one of the larger of the naval artillery installations built by the Germans during the Second World War. This one has been restored by the Channel Islands Occupation Society and is occasionally opened to the public.

The commemorative stone on the Noirmont headland was erected in memory of the people of Jersey who died during the Second World War.

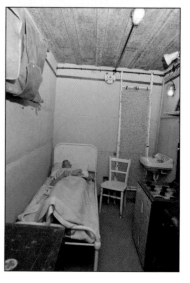

The range finder on the restored artillery installation at **Noirmont.**

Above
La Tour de Vinde, situated at the foot of Noirmont Point, is one of a series of 31 naval defence towers built around the coast between 1779 and 1835. Now painted black and white, it is used as a sea mark.

These and previous pages
Ile au Guerdain stands in the centre of Portelet Bay. The tower upon it is Janvrin's Tomb, the final resting place of Philippe Janvrin who, in 1721, died of the plague on his ship which was anchored in nearby Belcroute Bay. Fear of the illness did not permit his body to be brought ashore.

Ouaisné Bay.

The coast off **Portelet Common**.

Below **La Cotte**.

St Brelade's Bay is popular with tourists. As well as the sandy beach, one of Jersey's busiest during the summer, the area has numerous pretty walks and gardens. The parish church and Fisherman's Chapel add to the picturesque quality of the bay.

Next to St Brelade's Church, within the churchyard, is the **Fisherman's Chapel**. Although its precise age is unknown, excavations indicate that it dates from the late 12th century. It is renowned for its medieval wall paintings.

Just yards from the beach, this archway leads to **St Brelade's Church**, the closest in the Island to the sea.

A maze of tunnels covering some four acres, the **German Underground Hospital** in St Lawrence was built during the German occupation of the Island in the Second World War by a workforce that included Russian and Polish prisoners of war, many of whom died in the process. Many locals in the Island during the Occupation believed that gas chambers were being constructed for their eventual extermination. However, at the time of the Liberation of the Island in 1945, it was indeed a fully operational hospital.

The operating theatre in the German Underground Hospital at St Laurence.

The 'numbers' on the clock in the departure hall at Jersey Airport represent the crests of the Island's 12 parishes.

The state-of-the-art departure hall at Jersey Airport.

Jersey Airport was opened in 1937 and was recently refurbished to cope with increased passenger numbers.

The distinctive **British Airways** tailfins lined up at Jersey Airport.

flybe, formerly **British European**, and before that Jersey European, is a major carrier on the Jersey-UK routes. The airline was owned by the late Jack Walker, a Jersey resident.

As an international finance centre, Jersey's air links with UK and European cities are paramount.

British Airways fly several scheduled flights every day to a number of UK airports from the Island.

Beauport Bay, on the Island's south coast.

The **Railway Walk**, which leads through the Parish of St Brelade from St Aubin to Corbière, is a reminder of the days when trains were the main form of transport.

Corbière Lighthouse

Corbière Lighthouse, on the south-west corner of the Island, was built in 1873-4 and is believed to be the first lighthouse to be constructed in concrete. Prior to that a number of ships were wrecked off the rocky coastline. The lighthouse, which stands more than 100 ft above sea level, is accessible at low tide via a narrow causeway. However, the incoming tide quickly washes over the path and many visitors have found themselves stranded. In 1946 assistant lighthouse keeper Peter Larbalastier lost his life trying to save just such a soul.

Petit Port.

The treacherous rocks around **Corbière Lighthouse** led many ships to their peril.

Following pages

La Rocco tower in St Ouen's Bay – one of the series of 31 naval defence towers built around the Island's coast between 1779 and 1835. La Rocco was used for target practice by the Germans during the Second World War and was extensively damaged. However, major renovation managed to save it.

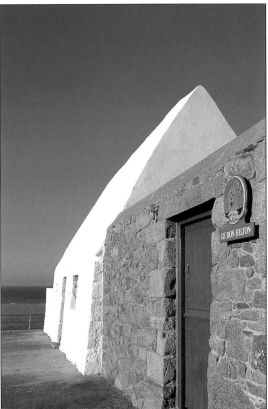

Le Don Hilton, also known as **La Caumine à Marie Best**, stands on the Five Mile Road, and is a familiar subject for artists.

A dry spring spells doom for potato growers. The **Jersey Royal** must be harvested early if it is to beat foreign competition – so farmers turn on the irrigation.

Following pages
St Ouen's Bay is the longest stretch of white sandy beach in Jersey and popular both with visitors and local people.

Local, national and international surfing championships are regularly held at St Ouen's Bay. The beach is also popular with enthusiasts of other watersports.

The spectacular view out across **St Ouen's Bay**.

Granite crosses to mark the Millennium were erected in the Island's 12 parishes. This one stands next to **St Ouen's Manor**.

While not as important a crop as they were in the 1970s and 1980s, daffodils are still grown in Jersey both for their flowers and their bulbs. The flowers are exported in chilled containers to UK wholesale markets and supermarket chains.

Concrete fortifications built by the Germans during the occupation still dominate the skyline around the coast.

The site of an Iron Age village, **Pinnacle Rock** is between L'Etacq and Grosnez.

On the headland above **Plémont**, the now-empty Pontin's Holiday Village sits on the skyline.

Plémont, on the north coast, is hailed by some as Jersey's most beautiful beach. Its white sand is completely covered at high tide.

Opposite page
Very little is known about the history of **Grosnez Castle**, other than that it was a ruin in the mid-16th century. Situated on a headland in the north-west corner of the Island at St Ouen, all that remains are the ruined gatehouse and the foundations of some small buildings. On a clear day you can see most of the other Channel Islands from Grosnez Point.

Grève de Lecq.

Devil's Hole is a natural archway in the cliff. The area is no longer accessible on the north coast.

The spectacular granite cliffs on the north coast stand over 400 feet above sea level. From many vantage points it is possible, on a clear day, to see the other Channel Islands and the French coast, including Cap de la Hague.

Following page
Grève de Lecq Bay and harbour in St Ouen.

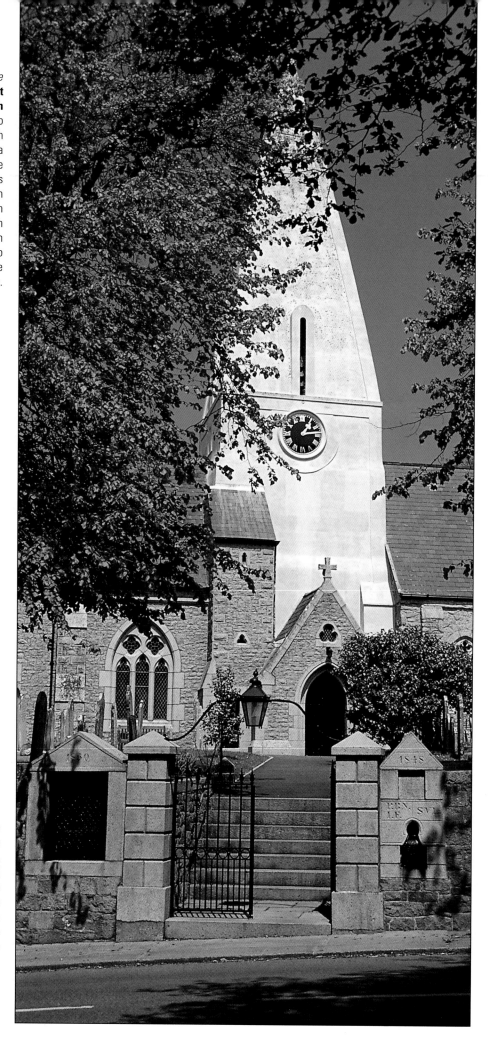

Previous page
The history of **St John's Church** goes back to 1150. Although the spires on a number of the parish churches have been rendered, that on St John's Church was removed in the early 1970s to reveal fine granitework.

Holy Trinity Church dates back to 1090. A piece of braid from one of the shoes worn at the execution of King Charles I is sealed into the altar pedestal. In latter years the church's stone spire has been rendered.

St John's Church

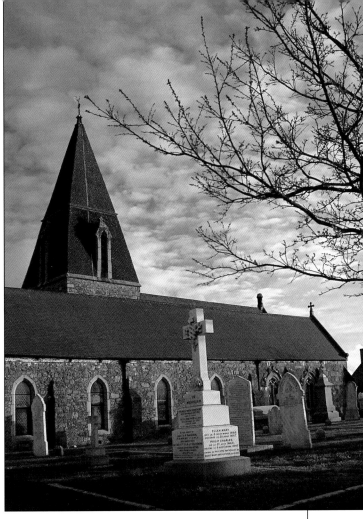

St Ouen's Parish Church

The parish church of **St Martin** or, to give it its correct title, **St Martin-the-Old** to distinguish it from St Martin de Grouville, dates back to 1042 and has an unusual number of buttresses supporting its walls, some of which are surmounted by stone figures.

Bonne Nuit is one of a number of pretty harbours on the north coast of the Island.

Jersey's French heritage lives on in its place names.

Sea angling is a popular pastime in Jersey. Mackerel, snipe (garfish), wrasse, grey mullet and bass are among the species you can hook.

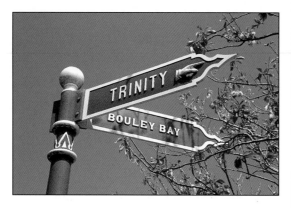

In recent years the Island's signposting has improved dramatically.

The hill leading up from **Bouley Bay** is used for racing – part of the British Motor Racing Hill Climb Championships.

With an abundance of crab and lobster in Jersey waters, many part-time fishermen drop lobster pots in the summer months.

Many small bays and inlets, some inaccessible, are dotted around Jersey's coastline.

This memorial, at **Trinity**, is to Captain Philip Ayton and his nine colleagues, who took part in one of the few commando raids on the Channel Islands during the German Occupation. Capt Ayton trod on a mine near Petit Port at Les Platons and later died in hospital of his injuries.

Opposite page
Lowland gorillas are one of the species that has been successfully bred at **Jersey Zoo**.

THIS MEMORIAL IS DEDICATED TO
THE BRITISH AND FRENCH COMMANDOS
WHO TOOK PART IN
OPERATION HARDTACK 28
ON
25.7 AND 26TH DECEMBER 1943,
THE COMMANDING OFFICER
CAPTAIN P. A. AYTON
WAS FATALLY WOUNDED DURING THE RAID

This giant stone dodo is a stark reminder to visitors to Jersey Zoo of what the work of the **Durrell Wildlife Conservation Trust** is all about – saving endangered species from extinction.

This sculpture of author and naturalist **Gerald Durrell** stands in the grounds of the world-famous Jersey Zoo, which he opened in 1959. The Durrell Wildlife Preservation Trust has been responsible for breeding programmes which have allowed endangered species to be raised and returned to their natural habitats. The Princess Royal is the Trust's patron.

Pink flamingos thrive in a natural environment at Jersey Zoo.

A friendly face at Rozel!

Fishermen's huts line Rozel Harbour.

Opposite page
Rozel is a small fishing harbour where part-time fishermen moor their boats and land their catches of crab and lobster. Concerted efforts have been made to resist calls for more car parking in the area with the result that Rozel remains virtually unspoilt.

St Catherine's Breakwater was built in the mid-19th century. The original intention was to form a naval harbour with a second breakwater stretching out from nearby Archirondel. However, on completion of the half-mile-long breakwater in 1855 at a cost to the Jersey taxpayers of £250,000, it was discovered that the 'harbour' was too shallow for naval warships, so the rest of the plan was abandoned. Today, St Catherine's is a popular walking spot for locals and visitors.

Brittany Ferries' vessel *Bretagne* making her way past the Island.

St Catherine's Breakwater.

'An obscure and very mysterious corner of the earth' is how Victor Hugo referred to **The Minquiers**, a group of islands just over 11 miles south-east of Jersey. Twice a year, when the tide falls very low, the Minquiers is actually bigger than Jersey, measuring in total some 19 miles by 11 miles. The islands are part of the Parish of Grouville.

Previous pages
The **Ecréhous** lie just over six miles off the coast of Jersey but are part of the Parish of St Martin. They comprise nine square miles of reefs and are a popular destination for local and French sailors. There are no permanent inhabitants on the reef, but there are houses on three islands in the group – Maître Ile, Blanche Ile and Marmotière. These are owned by Jersey residents and include an Impôt (Customs) post.

Only one island
on the Minquiers,
Maîtresse Ile, has
buildings on it.

St Catherine's Woods are a natural paradise for families.

La Chasse des Demoiselles Bandinel in St Martin is believed to be the longest road name in the Island.

One of the entrances to **St Martin's Churchyard**.

At **St Catherine's Bay** stands one of the defence towers built around the Island's coast between 1779 and 1835. The St Catherine's RNLI inshore lifeboat is housed in this cluster of buildings. The Island's main lifeboat station is at St Helier.

St Catherine's Bay with Archirondel Tower in the distance.

Opposite page Probably one of the most famous landmarks in Jersey is **Mont Orgueil** or **Gorey Castle**. It is believed to have been built around 1204 to protect the Island from French invasion. Gorey Pier, below it, is still an active harbour with small ferries bringing tourists from the nearby Normandy coast.

An aerial view of **Mont Orgeuil** clearly shows the vastness of the castle.

Sir Walter Raleigh, who was Governor of Jersey from 1600-1603, is said to have been fond of the castle and, according to the history books, it is largely down to him that it was retained.

A distinctive yellow Jersey public call box.

Previous pages
Gorey Harbour is a popular destination for tourists. In the 1800s several of the Island's 18 shipyards had a presence here. Gorey Pier was the terminus for the Eastern Railway.

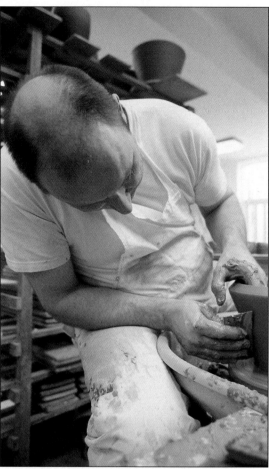

The **Jersey Pottery** was opened in 1948. Every item is produced on the premises. The Pottery has a thriving shop and many goods are exported overseas.

Visitors to the Jersey Pottery can see craftsmen at work at every stage of the production process.

Hand-painting is the hallmark of the items produced at the Jersey Pottery.

The **Royal Jersey** on **Grouville Common** is the Island's premier golf club, and six-times British and US Open champion Jerseyman Harry Vardon played here. This statue of him, which stands at the entrance to the club, was unveiled in 2001.

This lavoir or ancient washing place at Marais á La Cocque in Grouville is one of a number in the Island. The pump was a later addition in 1930. Both were renovated by the **Parish of Grouville** for the Millennium.

Opposite page
The 'village' area of the **Parish of Grouville**, which includes the parish church and parish hall.

Years of heated debate preceded the decision to flood Queen's Valley to provide another catchment area for water for the Island. Prior to the flooding, the valley was 'home' to television detective Jim Bergerac.

The Neolithic ritual site at **La Hougue Bie** is topped by a 40-ft high mound on top of which stand two chapels – Notre Dame de la Clarté, which was built in the 12th century, and the Jerusalem chapel and crypt built in 1520. A pilgrimage to the chapels takes place every year and several other services are held here.

Opposite page
As well as the Neolithic burial chamber, the site houses an **archaeological museum** and a **German Occupation museum**.

The burial tomb, which is part of the Neolithic ritual site at La Hougue Bie, dates back to about 3,000 BC. It is believed to be one of the finest of its kind in Western Europe.

Opposite page
Properties bordering the coast, such as these along the coast road at **Grouville**, are much sought after.

The world-famous Jersey breed of cattle originated in the Island. The purity of the breed has been guaranteed by a decision in 1789 to ban the importation of other breeds.

Mechanised harvesters can damage the delicate **Jersey Royal** potato, so some growers still prefer hand lifting. Seasonal labour is brought in to dig the crop, which remains the Island's premier export.

Seymour Tower stands about a mile and a quarter out in the Royal Bay of Grouville. It is possible to walk to it at low tide, but the sea comes in quickly and many people have drowned in the vicinity over the years.

The rocky coast line at **La Rocque**.

On 8th January 1781, the French troops who were to take part in the Battle of Jersey came ashore at La Rocque. This plaque was erected to mark their landing place.

Le Hocq.

They may look harmless, but the rocks on Jersey's east coast can be navigated only by the most experienced sailors.